Pulp Fiction

Perfect Paper Projects

D1109004

Pulp Fiction contains original content with content first published in 2011 by Design Originals in the first edition of the book by the same name.

Photography by Auxy Espinoza.

ISBN 978-1-57421-413-0

To learn more about the other great books from Design Originals
or to find a retailer near you, call toll-free 800-457-9112 or visit us at
www.d-originals.com.

Note to Authors: We are always looking for talented authors to write new books
in our area of crafts. Please send a brief letter
describing your idea to Acquisition Editor, 1970 Broad Street, East Petersburg, PA 17520.

Printed in Indonesia
First printing

Mark Montano

Pulp Fiction
Perfect Paper Projects

2ND EDITION

Design Originals

18

24

37

Contents

What you will learn

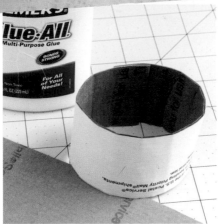

And so much more!

Introduction

Paper is my passion...my favorite medium. It is abundant, cheap, and there is so much you can do with it! Who would have thought that you could turn a pile of old magazine pages into earrings worthy of a New York modeling runway? I'll show you how to make jewelry that you'll be proud to wear and home decor that sparkles with personality. Together, we will make gifts worth giving.

I reveal secrets that professional designers use to create stunning results. I want you to have the confidence to present items that grab attention. When someone notices the glitter magnet on your fridge and asks, "Where did you find that?", you'll respond with pride— "I made it."

You know how I love anything recycled. I'll show you how to breathe new life into a battered briefcase, rescue a beleaguered table, turn a boring mirror into a spectacular room accent and create interesting objects for home decor. Let's create something wonderful together and spare the planet at the same time.

These projects offer inventive possibilities to custom fit your personal taste and I didn't leave out the fun. Imagine yourself celebrating Mardi Gras or welcoming the New Year wearing a fabulous feathered mask worthy of a Las Vegas show. All your friends will want one. Unleash your creativity with the kids. Experiment with unique puzzles, cards, notebooks, and envelope sets. Turn old Christmas card boxes into dimensional greetings.

I know you can do this. You can't mess it up—it's only paper and glue, a little paint, and a whole lot of imagination. Enjoy the process and let me know how it turns out. I'm available at *markmontanonyc@aol.com* and I love hearing about your crafting adventures.

Mark

Mark Montano

ARTIST • AUTHOR • TV HOST

When I was 7, we moved in to what would be our family home for the rest of my life. Five boys, a dog, two creative parents pulled up to a '70s style ranch house with five bedrooms, two baths and a 1-acre yard with trees that were perfectly placed for backyard baseball games. I remember that when we moved in, it seemed so empty and huge. I also remember my mother saying that with a little creativity it would be a home in no time. She was right.

You see, with five boys and a stay-at-home mom, we budgeted like any other family. When it was time to buy certain things, like a desk for my room, my grandfather made one for me from a box TV set. He removed the big glass screen, painted it jet black and added some very cool trim. I LOVED IT! The speakers on the side were my paperwork cubbyholes. When my mother found an old desk at the thrift store, she antiqued it with two different colors of beige and taupe and decoupaged gold roses above the handles. It was absolutely beautiful and it's still in her den today. Those are just two examples of the kinds of things that filled our home. Things that didn't cost a lot of money, but were as beautiful as any object in any beautiful home.

My aunts and grandmother taught me to sew as soon as I could hold a needle without poking my eye out. My grandfather was a carpenter who always had a boat halfway built in his back yard. My uncles were painters, carpenters, metal workers, you name it. I was surrounded by people who were creative my entire life and I loved it. I didn't know another way and I'm grateful for every scrap of wood and fabric.

When I was 12, I joined a Boy Scouts troop called the Koshare Indian Dancers. We learned traditional Sioux, Kiowa and Navajo dances, songs and costume making. I immediately took to the beading. I'm still not a very good dancer, but I learned so much from an incredible man named Buck, who taught us how to cut abalone shells, make breastplates, loin cloths and headdresses from pheasant feathers. In my little town I had found a place for my creative energy.

We did all of this based out of the Koshare Indian Museum, which is a traditional Kiva in La Junta, Colorado. Only as I look back do I realize how blessed I was to have had this experience. My dad still has all of the Peyote beadwork key chains I made for him.

When I was 14, my mom gave me a 1955 portable Singer sewing machine which I still have. I had been sewing on our old junky machine and it just wasn't doing the trick. My dad was actually the one who taught me to sew, oddly enough. He used to do upholstery as a side job and was really good at it. If I helped, I got the scraps of vinyl and that was good enough for me.

It was then I made the decision (at 14!) that I would go to college in NYC and become a fashion designer. What did I know? There were barely electric stoplights in our little corner of Colorado and a goal like that seemed impossible. But, that didn't stop me. I taught myself how to sew everything. I made my own tuxedo for my prom, made blouses for my mom and curtains for my room. You name it, I sewed it.

After high school, I headed to Colorado State University and then to FIT in New York City where I landed my first internship with Oscar de la Renta as an all-around servant to anyone who needed anything. I got coffee, picked up thread, delivered packages and helped cut garments when they needed an extra hand before the collections.

After graduation, I put together my first clothing collection and hauled it on my back to various stores in New York, one of which was Patricia Fields. She did all of the clothes for the *Sex and the City* movies. She was the first one to buy my collection and that's where my fashion career started. The Friday night before I had to deliver my first order, I had seven friends in my tiny apartment sewing on buttons, ironing and bagging. It was so exciting.

After two years of selling my collection to different stores, I opened my first store in the East Village of NYC. A few years later I won the Cotton Incorporated award and was able to show my first real runway collection at Bryant Park where all of the major designers showed. It was amazing and my real fashion career was in full swing. The next season I got compared to Calvin Klein in the New York Post and got the cover of the Style section of the *New York Times*.

Lots happened after that. I showed in the tents for 10 years, had two boutiques, became an editor at *CosmoGirl!* magazine,

a contributing editor at the *New York Post*, had a syndicated column, wrote books and enjoyed my creative life so much that some days I couldn't believe that I got to get up and make things for a living. I still feel that way.

One day I got a call to audition for a show called *While You Were Out* on TLC and I went. I got the job and said to myself, it's time to transition from fashion to interiors and get everything that I can out of this one life that I have. I still work in TV and get to make things every day for my books and shows and am so grateful for every scrap and every beat-up table and briefcase that comes into my workroom.

I guess what I'm trying to say as I write this is that being creative can enhance your life in ways that are absolutely AMAZING. Give in to your creative urges, nurture them, enjoy them and create something. At the same time you are creating something, you're creating a life, a history, a story, and an object that has meaning. That scarf you're making means something to the friend you're making it for.

The objects on these pages are going to mean something because you put your time and part of your soul into them. Make them, change them, give them away and make some more.

Just create and watch what happens.
—Mark

Bauhaus Bead Necklace

This is a terrific project for kids and those chic ladies who love big accessories. Here's something to think about when you're making this project: There are 350 million magazines published every year and the majority of them get tossed! Also, each person in the United States uses an average of one 100 foot tall Douglas fir in paper goods every year.

That's the only reason I need to make these beautiful paper bead necklaces.

YOU'LL NEED:

- ✦ Scissors
- ✦ Elmer's Glue
- ✦ Magazine pages
- ✦ Spray or acrylic paint (your choice)
- ✦ Beads to go in between your paper beads
- ✦ Shoebox lid
- ✦ Straight pins

HERE'S HOW:

1. Cut your magazine pages with the pattern provided on page 66.

2. Starting at the pointy end, curl the paper all the way to the end and then fasten together with a little bit of Elmer's Glue.

3. Hold between your fingers for a few seconds while it sets.

4. Repeat until you have tons of beads. One magazine can make about 300!

5. Stab straight pins into a piece of cardboard or a shoebox lid and place each bead on a pin. Take them outside to spray paint them! You could also hand paint them and let them dry on the pins. It's up to you.

6. String your beads with a large needle and embroidery thread in lengths long enough to fit over your head.

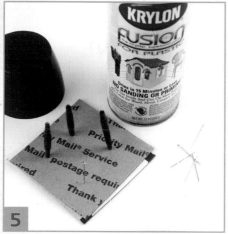

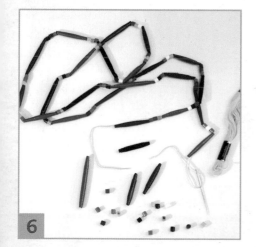

350 million magazines are published every year and the majority of them get tossed!

detail

Book Bead Bracelet

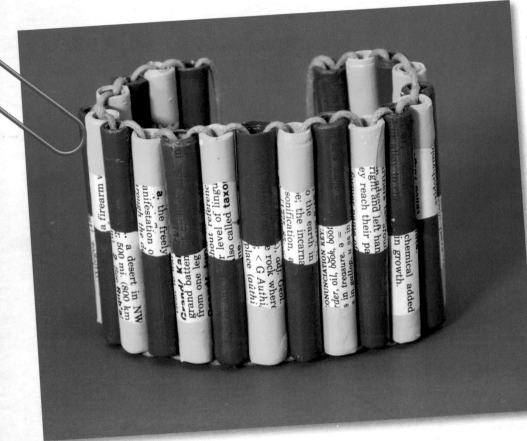

YOU'LL NEED:

- ✦ Book pages
- ✦ Drinking straws
- ✦ Transparent tape
- ✦ Elmer's Glue
- ✦ Acrylic paint in colors you like
- ✦ Paintbrushes
- ✦ 2 yards (180cm) of heavy duty cord
- ✦ 1 large lobster claw
- ✦ 1 jump ring
- ✦ Shoebox lid or cardboard
- ✦ Straight pins

detail

1

HERE'S HOW:

1. Cut your book pages in 2" (50mm) wide strips the length of your book.

2. Place a small piece of tape at the end of a strip and on the drinking straw and roll the book page around the straw.

3. Add some Elmer's Glue to the end to seal the bead.

4. Cut off the straw and start again until you have about 21 of these beads.

5. Poke some straight pins in a shoebox lid or some cardboard to create your drying board.

6. Paint each side of each bead and place on a pin to dry.

7. Thread your lobster claw and tie a knot around it in the middle of your cord exactly at the 1-yard mark.

8. Put one end of your cord through one end of a bead and the other end of the cord through the other end of a bead and pull until the string is taught.

9. Position the knot so it's centered against the center of this first bead.

10. Repeat step 3 until you've used all of your beads.

11. Once the last bead is in place, tie your cord in a very secure knot around a jump ring.

12. Cut the excess cord and tuck the ends inside the last bead (you might want to dab some glue on the ends to keep them in place) or let the strings hang loose for a more casual look.

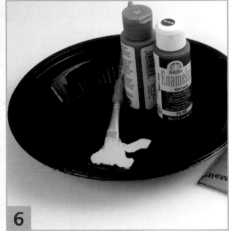

6

7

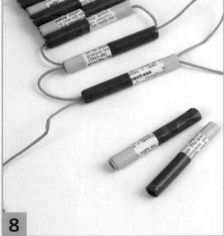

8

11

Bugle Bead Bracelet

I'm still experimenting with these bracelets and I keep finding new ways to make them. This is one of my favorites. The entire bracelet is made from discarded paper!

I think that's reason enough to be proud to wear it.

YOU'LL NEED:

✦ Magazine pages

✦ Newspaper pages

✦ Cardboard

✦ Scissors

✦ Elmer's Glue

✦ Hot glue gun

✦ Spray paint in army green

✦ Metallic gold marker pen

✦ Glitter Blast in Bronze Blaze

✦ Shoebox lid

✦ Straight pins

HERE'S HOW:

1. Cut a cardboard strip 9" by 2" (230mm by 50mm).

2. Rub your cardboard along the edge of the table to give it a curve—just like you would curling a ribbon, but instead of scissors, you're using a table edge.

3. Overlap either 1" (25mm) or ½" (15mm) depending on your bangle size and glue together so that the glued cuff is the same size as one of your other bracelets.

4. Slightly water down some Elmer's Glue and start gluing on small strips of magazine pages or newspaper. Use several layers to create a very sturdy cuff.

5. Cut your magazine pages with the pattern provided on page 66.

6. Starting with the pointy end, curl the paper all the way to the end and then fasten together with a little bit of Elmer's Glue.

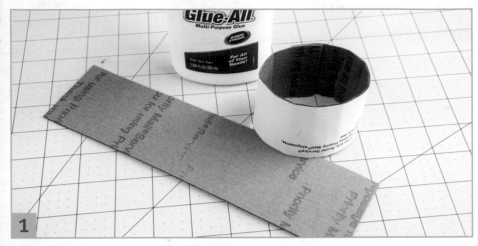

1

3

4

6

7. Hold the bead between your fingers for a few seconds while it sets. Repeat until you have enough beads to circle your cuff.

8. Hot glue the beads around the cuff and add a bit more Elmer's Glue for good measure; let dry for a few hours. This would be a good time to start another one.

9. When dry, spray paint the cuff green outside and let dry.

10. Go in between each bead and around the edges with the metallic gold marker pen.

11. Glitter blast the edges with the Bronze Blaze and let dry.

8

Catalog Party Balls

I love tissue paper balls because they are magical. You unfold them and they make these light wonderful shapes; they look amazing hanging in clusters. I always wondered how they were made so one night I decided I was going to make my own and this is what I came up with after about 20 attempts!

YOU'LL NEED:

✦ Small catalog with about 30 pages (I like my Crate and Barrel mini catalogs)

✦ Elmer's Glue

✦ Hot glue gun

✦ Craft knife

✦ Cutting mat

✦ Scissors

✦ Marker

✦ 1 yard (90cm) of ribbon per ball

HERE'S HOW:

1. Make a 7" (20cm) diameter circle pattern and cut it exactly in half.

2. Divide the half circle into six equal pie slices and make them along the curved edge of your half circle. You will have five notches. This is your pattern.

3. Remove all of the cardboard and flyers from inside the catalog. You only want the pages.

4. Placing the straight edge of the pattern on the fold of the catalog, trace the half circle and the notches on the cover of the mini catalog.

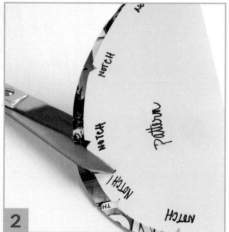

5. Carefully cut the magazine into a half circle with your craft knife. This will take a bit so be patient.

6. With your scissors, notch where you marked your notches.

7. Starting in between the first and second page of the catalog you will put a dot of glue on every other notch like you see in the photo.

8. Turn the page and put a dot of glue on the notches that were not glued on the previous page.

9. Continue alternating glue dots on notches until you reach the end.

10. Keep the catalog closed for about one-half hour until your glue dries.

11. Unfold your catalog ball and glue the front and back cover together with hot glue.

12. Attach a ribbon in the center with a bit more hot glue and hang.

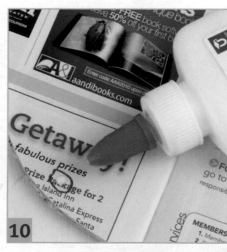

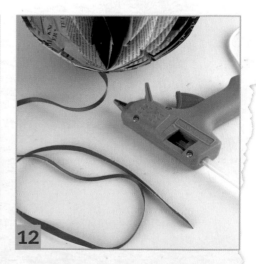

Magazine Mobile

This magazine mobile is graceful and elegant, and I'm sure everything you need to make it is stored under your sink. I have my mobile hanging in the kitchen window and every day I find myself staring at it and feeling very peaceful.

YOU'LL NEED:

- ✦ Magazines
- ✦ Scissors
- ✦ Stapler
- ✦ Elmer's Glue
- ✦ Needle and thread
- ✦ Medium-gauge wire
- ✦ Wire cutters

detail

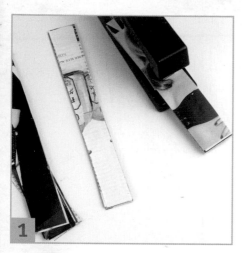

HERE'S HOW:

1. To make the magazine flowers, cut twelve strips of 1" by 6" (50mm by 150mm) magazine pages and staple them together exactly in the center. You will need to make seven of these.

2. Carefully bend (without creasing) the end of each strip down to the crease near the staple and add a dab of glue to keep it in place and continue with all twenty-four ends.

3. Cut two pieces of wire that are 6" (15cm) long and one that is 9" (25cm) long and bend a loop in the middle and at the end of each piece using your needle-nose pliers.

4. Tie thread around the center loop of your larger looped metal piece and hang it somewhere you can work.

5. Tie a double strand of thread 10" (25cm) long around the center of each of the other two looped metal pieces and hang one from each of the end loops of the larger looped wire.

6. Thread your needle with 14" (35cm) of thread (double strand) and push it through the center of one of the petals of your magazine flower and tie the end on one of the loops.

7. Continue until you have your flowers hanging like you see in the beauty shot.

8. *The length of the thread is up to you, but I like using from 9" to 12" (25cm to 30cm) per flower so the flowers are all at different levels.

I have my mobile hanging in the kitchen window and every day I find myself staring at it and feeling very peaceful.

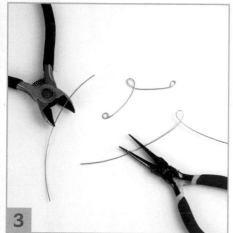

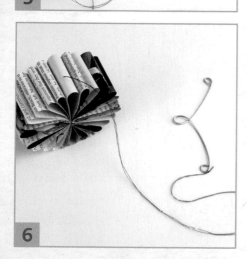

Masquerade Mask with Feathers

Is there anything more fun than showing up at a costume party and hanging out with people who don't know it's you? I can pull it off until I start to laugh and then everyone knows it's me. I love the simplicity and elegance of this mask. I also love the fact that I can make it from things I have hanging around my craft house.

YOU'LL NEED:

- ✦ Cardboard
- ✦ Elmer's Glue
- ✦ Book pages
- ✦ 4' (120cm) of ribbon of your choice
- ✦ Small gauge wire and wire cutters
- ✦ Rhinestones
- ✦ Hole punch
- ✦ 1 yard (90cm) of trim
- ✦ X-Acto knife
- ✦ Scissors
- ✦ Hot glue gun and glue sticks
- ✦ Mod Podge Gloss

HERE'S HOW:

1. Cut out the mask pattern in cardboard and slightly bend it in a curve. Try it on your face for size and comfort.

2. Trace your mask pattern on two book pages and cut out. These will be used to cover the front and the back. You could also use smaller pieces of book pages and collage them on your cardboard. It's up to you.

3. Using Elmer's white glue that's been watered down a little bit, glue the pages to the front and back of the mask. Because the mask will be a tiny bit wet from the glue, bend your mask so that it fits comfortably around your face and set it between two items to dry.

4. Now that the mask has dried and hardened, you can either leave it plain or paint it. To give it a diamond pattern like I did in the photograph, carefully draw crisscross lines about 1" (25mm) apart at 45° angles going in both directions. Fill in every other diamond with watered down acrylic paint and let dry.

5. Once the layers are dry, coat the mask in Mod Podge. This will make it nice and sturdy.

6. When dry, hot glue your trim around the mask and around the eyes.

7. For each feather, you will take one book page and fold it in half.

8. Spread a layer of Elmer's Glue on one half.

9. Insert an 8" (20cm) piece of wire between the pages and seal it. Let dry.

10. When fully dry, cut out your feather shape and carefully cut the feather as shown

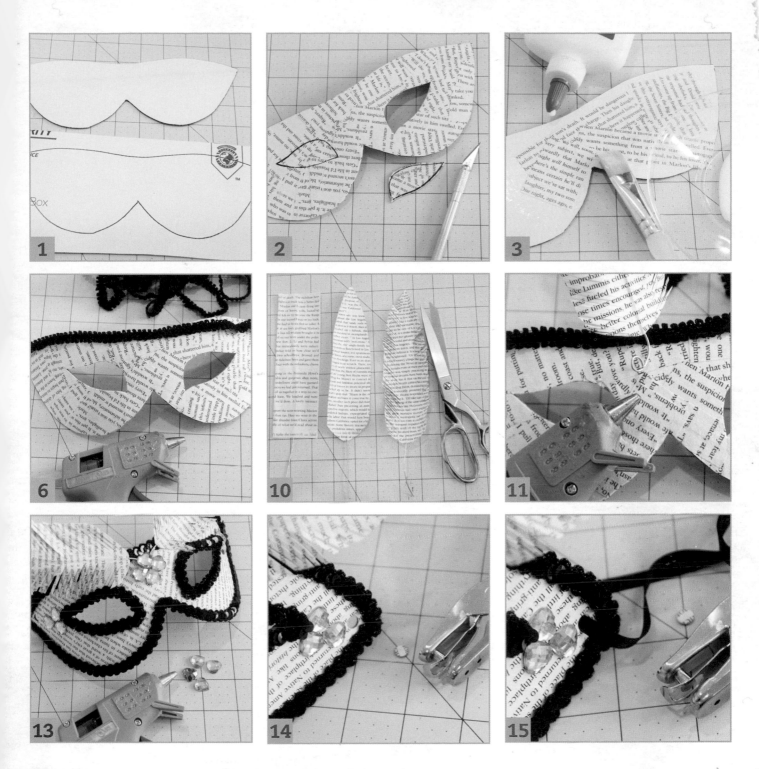

11. Position the feathers on the center of the mask and hot glue in place.

12. When dry, bend into shape.

13. Using your hot glue gun, add the rhinestones.

14. Punch a hole on each end of your mask.

15. String the ribbon through and tie a knot if you want.

✳ See project patterns on page 77.

Book Page and Butterfly Table

If you want to make something look antique, cover it in really old book pages. Well, at least that's what I discovered when making this table. This project uses a double-print process that you can easily do at a copy shop such as Staples. Once you learn how to do it you'll be using this double print process for everything. It's addictive.

YOU'LL NEED:

- ✦ Simple table that needs some love
  (Mine was a LACK table from Ikea)

- ✦ Images you like
  (I chose butterflies)

- ✦ Book pages

- ✦ Access to a laser copy machine
  (The ink from your home copier will run.)

- ✦ Plaid Mod Podge

- ✦ 1" (25mm) paintbrush

- ✦ Elmer's Glue

Size: 22" x 22"
(560mm x 560mm)

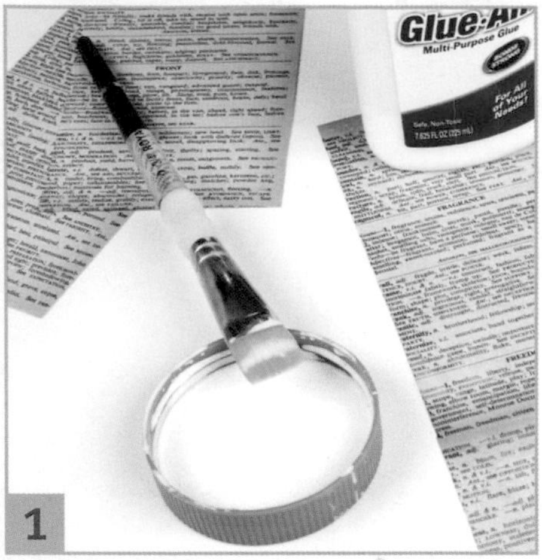

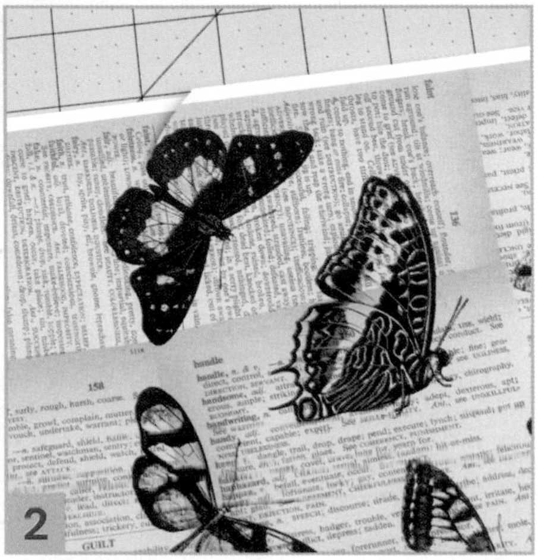

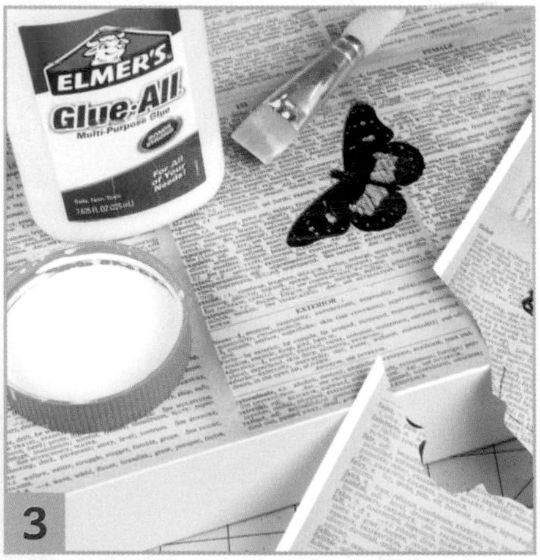

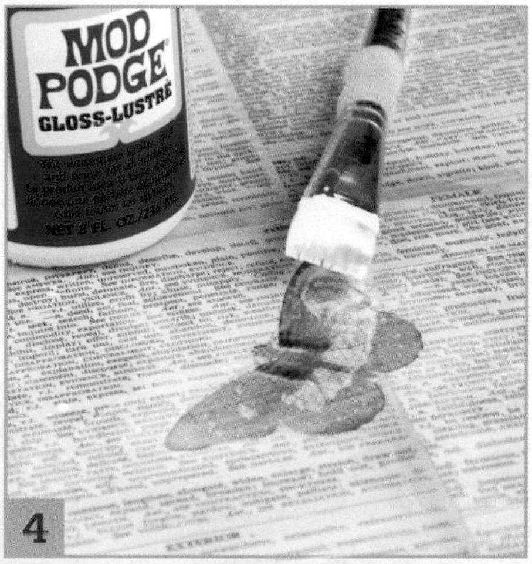

HERE'S HOW:

1. Water down the glue just a bit so that it's easy to spread. Carefully adhere your pages to every square inch of your table. If you use full book pages, it will take much less time and give a terrific effect.

2. Place several book pages on a color copy machine, making sure you fill up the entire page. Make 5 copies and take them to a regular Black and White copy machine. Load the copied book pages face down in the paper stack. Put your butterfly images (or the images you're using) on the copy machine and copy them on top of the copied book pages. This is my secret double print technique.

3. Cut out these images and paste them on top of your book covered table.

4. Cover the entire table with Mod Podge for a protected finish.

❋ Use artwork on page 70 or create your own!

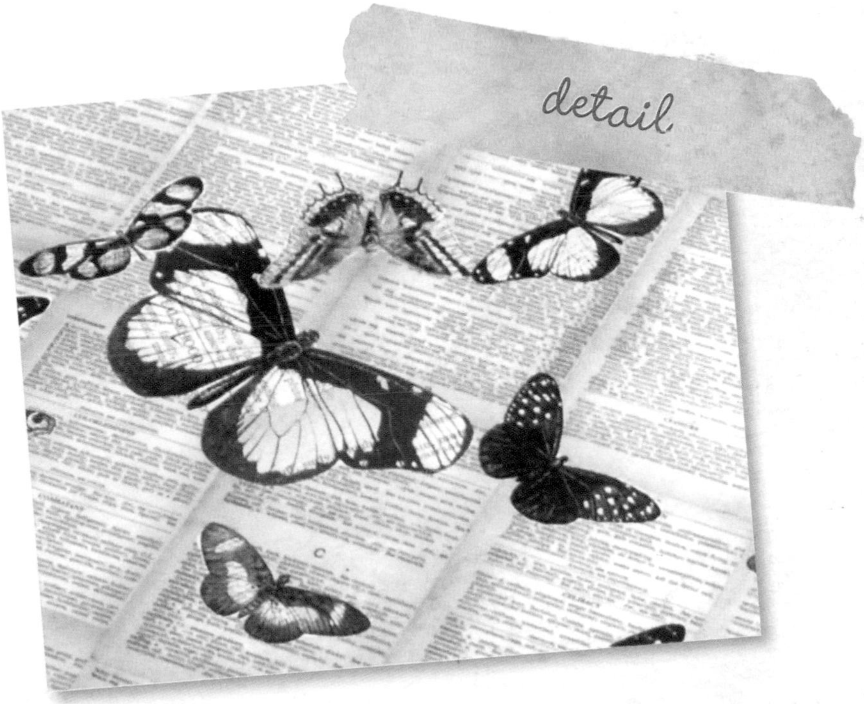

My Secret Double-Print Process

3-D Greeting Card Box

I'm not sure if you're like me, but I can't toss out any kind of box. I'm a box hoarder and the TLC network may show up at my house very soon to find me. I particularly love greeting card boxes—you know, the ones with the clear plastic top. I used one of these boxes for this project and couldn't be happier with it. I liked it so much, in fact, that I sent it to myself for my birthday because I couldn't bear to part with it. Is that so wrong?

YOU'LL NEED:

- ✦ One greeting card box with clear lid
- ✦ Book pages
- ✦ Twigs
- ✦ Two 1" x 5" (25mm x 125mm) plain papers
- ✦ Calligraphy pen and ink
- ✦ Butterfly stamp
- ✦ Gold embossing powder and embossing gun
- ✦ Embossing ink pad
- ✦ Scissors
- ✦ Krylon Metallic Gold spray paint
- ✦ Elmer's Glue

SIZE: 5" x 7" x 1" (125mm x 175mm x 25mm) deep

detail

HERE'S HOW:

1. Cut your book pages in small pieces and glue them inside the box with some slightly watered down glue.

2. Break your twigs so they fit in your box and then spray paint them Gold.

3. Stamp your book pages with a butterfly using embossing ink. Cover the stamp with embossing powder and set with a heat gun.

4. Cut out the butterflies and pinch the center so they are dimensional (not just flat).

5. Write the greeting on the 1" x 5" (25mm x 125mm) paper using a calligraphy pen. Let the ink dry.

6. Roll the edges at a bit of a slant.

7. Glue twigs in the box, then your greeting and finally your butterflies.

8. Cover with the plastic lid.

✱ Use artwork on page 70 or create your own!

Standing Cards

I like creating cards that people really like to display once they open the envelope. I'm not sure about you, but those cards with cartoon illustrations just end up in the dresser.

These standing cards end up staying out in full view for quite a while and the recipient thinks about you every time they see it! Making this card marries my two favorite crafting processes: my love for cereal and my love for putting book pages through my copy machine.

YOU'LL NEED:

- ✦ Image you want to copy
- ✦ Cardboard from a cereal box
- ✦ Book pages
- ✦ Ruler
- ✦ Craft knife
- ✦ Elmer's Spray Mount

Size: 4" x 6"
(100mm x 150mm)

HERE'S HOW:

1. Choose the image you want to use for your card. I find most anything works but you might have to experiment a little bit.

2. Copy the image onto 1 book page of an average size book (about 5" x 8") (125mm x 200mm).

3. Cut out some rectangles in cardboard from a cereal box. This cardboard works perfectly for this project.

4. Apply spray mount to the back of your image and stick it to the printed side of a cereal box card.

5. Draw a line ⅝" (15mm) around the image but not across the bottom.

6. Lightly mark at the half point of the card where it will be folded.

7. Cut your image out, leaving the frame intact and leaving the bottom of the image connected.

8. Lightly score across the frame in the center where you marked and fold the card in half so that it can stand on its own.

Standing Cards End Up Staying Out in Full View

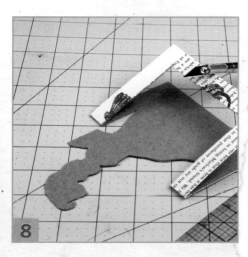

I'm Puzzled

My neighbor Denise is 13 and she gave me total approval to do this puzzle. She loves cutting out pictures from magazines and making art. I guess what I'm trying to say is that 13-year-old girls and I have a lot in common and that's why I'm puzzled. You can use any images for this project. It could be really fun to make a birthday greeting or a letter.

detail

YOU'LL NEED:

✦ 1 piece of 10" x 14" (25cm x 35cm) cardboard

✦ 1 piece of 8 ¾" x 12 ¾" (20cm x 30cm) cardboard

✦ Images from several magazines

✦ Copy machine

✦ Craft knife

✦ Scissors

✦ Cutting mat

✦ Elmer's Spray Adhesive (Optional: You'll need this if you copy your original art and mount it to cardboard)

✦ Elmer's Glue

SIZE: 9" x 13" (225mm x 330mm)

You can do this puzzle different ways. Use your original artwork for the puzzle or simply take your original art to the copy shop and make copies to use for your puzzle—it's up to you.

HERE'S HOW:

1. Cut ½" (15mm) squares out of the corners of the 10" x 14" (25cm x 35cm) cardboard.

2. Score on one side of the cardboard so you can fold up each edge ½" (15mm) to create a structure that looks like a box lid. This will contain your puzzle.

3. Cut out your magazine images.

4. Using a paintbrush, lightly coat each image with glue and adhere it to your 8¾" x 12¾" (20cm x 30cm) cardboard. Optional: You can use the original art for your puzzle piece or color copy your masterpiece at a copy shop. I like to color copy my art so that I can make more puzzles. If you choose to color copy your original artwork, you need to enlarge it a little bit. Use spray adhesive to mount it to your 8¾" x 12¾" (20cm x 30cm) piece of cardboard.

5. Once your artwork is done and mounted (either copied or using the original) carefully cut your puzzle pieces on a cutting mat. Cut in one direction first so your puzzle is in strips.

6. Cut each strip into smaller pieces.

7. Optional: Paint your puzzle container or cover it in extra art from your project for a terrific presentation. I covered the outside edges of my box in extra pieces from my color copies.

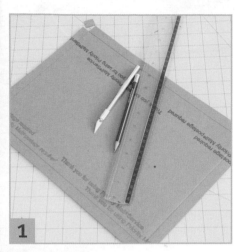

1

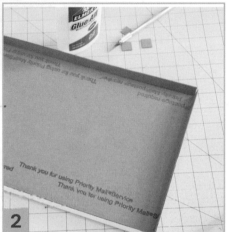

2

3

4

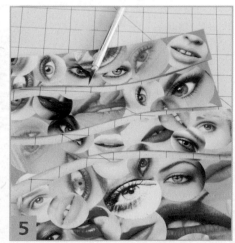

5

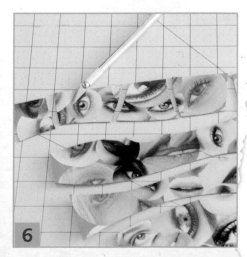

6

Magazine Mirror or Frame

I have to say I don't know anyone who doesn't have a similar frame in their home. If you don't have one, fret not because almost any frame or mirror will do. The Malma Mirror from Ikea is great for all kinds of projects and they are not expensive. In fact, they are quite cheap and can be used for all manner of crafty mayhem.

YOU'LL NEED:

- ✦ Mirror, frame or flat framed mirror
- ✦ Newspaper
- ✦ Magazines
- ✦ Buttons in the same size
- ✦ Krylon spray paint in your color choice
- ✦ Brush on Metallic Gold paint.
- ✦ Paintbrush
- ✦ Masking tape
- ✦ Elmer's Glue

SIZE: 10" x 10" (25cm x 25cm)

detail

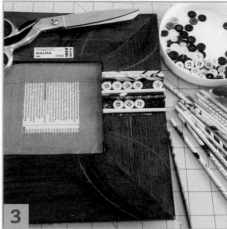

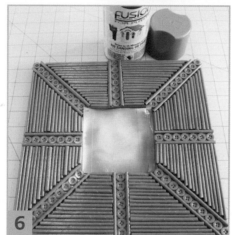

HERE'S HOW:

1. Cut magazine pages into 150 rectangles 3" x 6" (75mm x 150mm).

2. Roll them at a slant into tubes and glue the ends with a tiny dot of glue so they stay in place. I do this while watching a movie because it takes some time.

3. Decide what your design will be on the mirror and start gluing the buttons first. This will be a guide for your paper tubes.

4. Cut the tubes to size and glue them down.

5. Once your frame is covered in tubes and buttons, tape over the mirror part (or remove the glass if you're using a frame).

6. Coat it in spray paint. Let dry for 10 minutes. Spray several coats of paint, waiting 10 minutes in between coats. Let dry.

7. Lightly brush over your mirror with the metallic paint to give it a glint of glam.

Sewn Flower Brooch and Cuff

I will toss anything under the sewing machine to get some texture going. I love sewn book pages and while making some simple stationery with paper and the sewing machine, I began experimenting and these flowers just happened. A little Mod Podge and they were turning into fun paper jewelry before my very eyes.

YOU'LL NEED:

- ✦ Cardboard
- ✦ Newspaper
- ✦ Rhinestones
- ✦ Plaid Mod Podge Luster
- ✦ High Gloss Black spray paint
- ✦ Sewing machine with Black thread

- ✦ 1" (25mm) wide paintbrush
- ✦ Hot glue and glue gun
- ✦ Elmer's Glue

SIZE: 2" x 8½"
(50mm x 215mm) for cuff,
3½" (90mm) for brooch

1

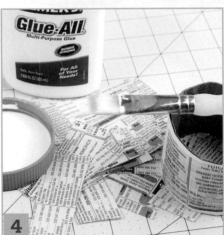

4

5

HERE'S HOW TO MAKE A BRACELET:

1. Create your bangle by cutting a piece of cardboard 2" x 9" (50mm x 230mm).

2. Run it along the side of the table so that it has a curve to it. You're curling the cardboard like you would a piece of curling ribbon but instead of using a scissor, you're using the edge of a table.

3. Glue it in a cuff shape, adjusting the size to slip over your hand.

4. Using some slightly watered down Elmer's Glue, cover the bangle with strips of newspaper. Give it several layers. The more layers you use, the more sturdy your cuff will be. Let it dry overnight.

5. Spray paint it with several coats of the Black high gloss, making sure to let it dry in between coats. Drying time is usually about 10 minutes. Let dry.

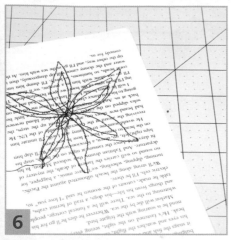

6

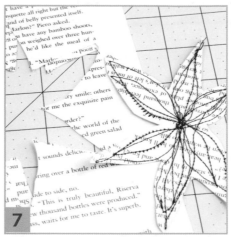

7

7

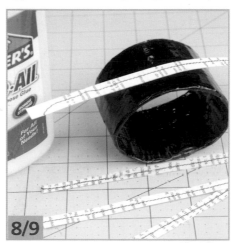

8/9

10

11

12

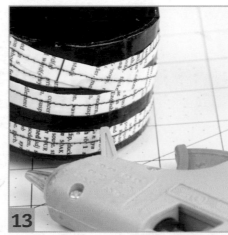

13

FOR THE FLOWER AND CUFF

6. Sew 2 layers of newspaper in the shapes of flowers on your sewing machine. Do this free form and have fun!

7. Cut out the flowers and coat them with several layers of Mod Podge on both sides, letting it dry in between coats. Do this several times so that they are really sturdy and hard. It may take 3 or 4 thick coats of the Mod Podge.

8. Optional: For the sewn strips around the cuff, sew straight lines on newspaper and cut it into strips that are about ⅜" (10mm) wide.

9. Glue the sewn strips around the cuff with Elmer's Glue. Let dry.

10. Cover with Mod Podge.

11. Adhere flowers together with hot glue.

12. Decorate the flower centers with rhinestones.

13. Hot glue the flower to the bangle.

✳ See project pattern on page 77.

Vogue Bracelets

Depending on the design and colors you choose, a bangle bracelet is versatile in style and taste. Plus, let's face it… it's paper and paint! How cool is that?

Depending on the lace pattern you choose, this cuff can have either a punk attitude or a very delicate feel. It's up to your own personal taste. I used hot pink, black and white because it gave it an edgy look, but color combinations like red, white and blue or yellow and black could be stunning. Come on, I know you can make this project.

YOU'LL NEED:

+ Cardboard
+ Strips of newspaper
+ Plaid Mod Podge Gloss
+ Elmer's Glue
+ Scissors
+ Craft knife
+ Krylon spray paint (Gloss Black, Pink, White)

SIZE: 3" x 8½"
(75mm x 215mm) and
1" x 8½" (25mm x 215mm)

HERE'S HOW:

FOR THE CUFF BRACELET

Follow steps 1–5 on pages 32–33.

LACE PATTERN BRACELET - Cut 3" (75mm) strips for the cuff.

1. Place your lace over the top and lightly coat it with the White spray paint. Let dry.

2. Match up your lace on the White and move it over just a bit and spray it with the Hot Pink. Let dry.

3. Coat the entire cuff in Mod Podge for a beautiful finished look.

ROLLED BANGLE BRACELET - Cut 1" (25mm) strips for the cuff.

4. Grab the end of the tube with the tip of the pliers and twist the tube around it to create a disk. Squeeze a dot of Elmer's Glue on the end to keep it in place.

5. Make disks in different sizes by adding tubes to make them bigger.

6. Hot glue disks to your bracelet in a design you like.

7. Spray paint with Gloss Black.

8. Cover with Mod Podge to give it a glossy finish.

Spark it up with some rhinestones dotted over the top to make your bracelets something special!

Pleats and Pearls

My great grandmother lived in a little gray house on the outskirts of town when I was growing up. Everything was filled with these wonderful cold grays, burgundies, blacks and whites—what I think of as a classic 1940 color scheme. In her living room she had small ceramic vases which were women's faces and torsos. I was fascinated by them, truly. One of them had this fantastic, tiny round brooch with pearls in the center. It's an old-fashioned feel that reminds me of my tiny and fabulous great grandmother.

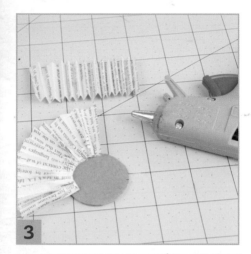

YOU'LL NEED:

- ✦ Book pages
- ✦ Cardboard
- ✦ Pearls
- ✦ Glitter glue
- ✦ Scissors
- ✦ Jewelry pin back
- ✦ Plaid Mod Podge Gloss
- ✦ Paintbrushes for Mod Podge
- ✦ Krylon spray paint (Ivory, Gold Metallic)
- ✦ Hot glue gun and glue sticks
- ✦ Elmer's Glue
- ✦ E-6000 craft adhesive

SIZE: 3" (75mm) diameter

HERE'S HOW:

1. Cut a disk out of cardboard that is a bit bigger than the size of a quarter.

2. Cut a book page in strips that are 1 ¼" (30mm) wide and as long as the book.

3. Accordion pleat the strips with ¼" (5mm) folds. Make 4.

4. Smash the edge of the pleated paper and hot glue it around the disk of cardboard.

5. Spray paint the pleated disk in Ivory. Let dry.

6. Lightly spray the edges of the pleated disk in Gold. If you mess up, just paint it Ivory and try again. Let dry.

7. Fill the center with Elmer's Glue and pearls and let dry for a few hours.

8. Add some glitter glue to the pearls where they meet.

9. Start coating the pleated edges with Mod Podge Gloss using a small paintbrush.

10. Coat the pleats several times on both sides until the paper is thick and sturdy.

11. Adhere a pin back using E-6000.

Honeycomb Cuffs

HERE'S HOW:

FOR THE CUFF BRACELET

Follow steps 1–4 on pages 32–33

FOR YOUR HONEYCOMB SHAPES

1. Cut magazine pages in rectangles that are about 6" x 12" (15cm x 30cm).

2. Roll the pages so they are 6" (15cm) long like a fat straw and glue down the end. I find rolling them around a pencil very helpful. Make about 25 of these. Let the glue dry.

3. Cut the rolled straw in pieces that are about ⅜" (10mm) long. The ends are going to pinch and they will form a leaf shape but don't worry, that's what you want. The lengths will vary.

HONEYCOMB BRACELET - Cut 3" (75mm) strips for the cuff.

4. Let cuff dry. Start gluing ⅜" (10mm) pieces all the way around.

5. Daub more glue on top of them where they meet. You really want to make sure this is sturdy.

ROLLED SHAPES BRACELET - Cut 1" (25mm) strips for the cuff.

6. Let cuff dry. Glue rolled shapes (page 4) all the way around.

PAINT THE BRACELET

7. Let dry. Paint with some Mod Podge around the edges, the inside and everywhere you can get it. Let dry.

8. Spray paint with the colors you've chosen by hitting the cuff randomly.

9. After it's covered in several coats of spray paint, use a paint brush to daub the acrylic paint on the top. Use all different colors.

10. If you have to go back with the spray paint, that's ok!

11. Cover with Mod Podge.

YOU'LL NEED:

+ Newspaper
+ Magazine pages
+ Krylon Spray paints in different colors
+ Plaid Mod Podge
+ Acrylic Paints in several different colors
+ Artist brushes
+ Pencil
+ Scissors
+ Elmer's Glue

SIZE: 2" x 8½" (50mm x 215mm)

Rolled Shapes

HERE'S HOW

1. Cut magazine pages into 1½" x 11" (40mm x 280mm) strips. Roll them into tubes and glue the ends with a tiny dot of Elmer's Glue.

2. Grab the end of the tube with the tip of the pliers and twist the tube around it to create a disk. Squeeze a dot of Elmer's Glue on the end to keep it in place.

3. Make disks in different sizes by adding tubes. Let dry.

YOU'LL NEED:

+ Magazine pages
+ Scissors
+ Needle-nose pliers
+ Elmer's Glue

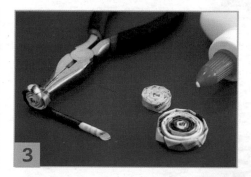

Blue Cuff

These bangles are meant to get people's attention and start them asking questions right awaay.

YOU'LL NEED:

+ Cardboard
+ Strips of newspaper
+ Magazine pages
+ Krylon Light Blue spray paint
+ Metallic Gold paint
+ Plaid Mod Podge Gloss
+ Small paintbrushes

+ Scissors
+ Craft knife
+ Needle-nose pliers
+ Elmer's Glue
+ Hot glue gun and glue sticks

SIZE: 2" x 8½" (50mm x 215mm)

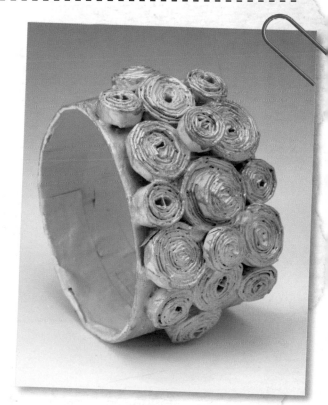

HERE'S HOW

FOR THE CUFF BRACELET
Follow steps 1–4 on page 32.
Cut 2" (50mm) strips for the cuff.

ROLLED SHAPES BLUE BRACELET

1. Hot glue disks to your bracelet in a design you like.

2. Spray paint and dust with the Metallic Gold paint.

3. Cover with Mod Podge to give it a glossy finish.

Vogue Leaf Earrings

When I was a fashion designer in New York City and living on a budget in the East Village, I had to make sure that the jewelry used on my runway shows was, well, show-stopping. Often I had to make my own jewelry to get the look that I wanted. I made these earrings much bigger for a show I did in 1994 and they were a hit. I sprayed them gold and from a distance they looked like real gold earrings!

Take this honeycomb concept and go crazy with it. It makes fantastic Christmas ornaments (see page 40) or even a terrific brooch. Come on, it's just paper and a little time.

YOU'LL NEED:

- ✦ Magazine pages
- ✦ Large jump ring
- ✦ Earring wires
- ✦ Plaid Mod Podge
- ✦ Krylon Metallic Gold spray paint (optional)
- ✦ Pencil
- ✦ Scissors
- ✦ Elmer's Glue

SIZE: 1" x 2" (25mm x 50mm)

HERE'S HOW:

MAKE HONEYCOMB SHAPES

1. Cut your magazine pages in rectangles that are about 6" x 12" (150mm x 300mm).

2. Roll the pages so they are 6" long like a fat straw and glue down the end. Let the glue dry. I find rolling them around a pencil very helpful. Make about 8 of these.

3. Cut the straw-shaped roll into pieces about ⅜" (10mm) long. The ends are going to pinch and they will form a leaf shape, but don't worry, that's what you want. Also, the sizes will vary and that's ok, too.

ASSEMBLE HONEYCOMB EARRINGS

4. With more Elmer's, glue them together side by side creating your shape. You could do any shape really, I let mine happen organically. Important: The top leaf loop should be a little less than ¼" (5mm) so that you can get your jump ring through it later.

5. Cover these with Mod Podge so that they have some strength.

6. Optional: Paint with Metallic Gold and let dry if you want some color.

7. Put your jump ring through the top leaf loop and attach the earring wire. You're ready to be the belle of the ball!

detail

Fashionista Earrings on a Budget

Honeycomb Ornaments

Being the creative dynamo you are, I'm sure you can come up with many other items to make with this process. I really like delicate looking and beautiful ornaments and I could make them for hours on end.

I find it relaxing and I love that it really only takes an old magazine and some glue to achieve such a wonderful look. Just pop in a good movie and see how relaxing this process can be. I was surprised at how sturdy these were when they were finished, too!

Creative Dynamo Ornaments
Made with Magazine Circles!

YOU'LL NEED:

✦ Magazine pages

✦ Sulyn Silver glitter

✦ Krylon Metallic Gold spray paints (Gold or Silver)

✦ Clear filament (fishing line)

✦ Pencil

✦ Scissors

✦ Plate

✦ Elmer's Glue

SIZE: 5" x 5" (125mm x 125mm)

detail

HERE'S HOW:

MAKE HONEYCOMB SHAPES

1. From magazine pages, cut 25 rectangles that are about 6" x 12" (15cm x 30cm).

2. Roll 1 piece of 6" x 12" (150mm x 305mm) around a pencil and glue down the end to make a fat 6" (150mm) long straw. Using a pencil is very helpful in this process. Make 25 of these. Let the glue dry.

3. Cut the rolls in pieces ⅜" (10mm) long. If the lengths slightly vary, that's ok. Pinch the ends, forming a leaf shape.

ASSEMBLE THE ORNAMENTS

4. Start gluing the pieces side by side creating a snowflake pattern. If you put some glue on a plate, you can just dip them in the glue and it goes much faster.

5. When you've created your shape, let it dry.

6. Spray paint the entire shape Silver or Gold

7. Paint glue on one side of your ornament and sprinkle with glitter. Repeat on the other side.

8. Add a loop of clear filament (fishing line) as a hanger.

Spider Magnets

There is nothing scarier than a spider, right? Well, not if it's covered in glitter. Actually, anything covered in glitter automatically loses its fright factor. These are so easy to make that you'll want to make several and leave them all over the house. I particularly like them on my fridge.

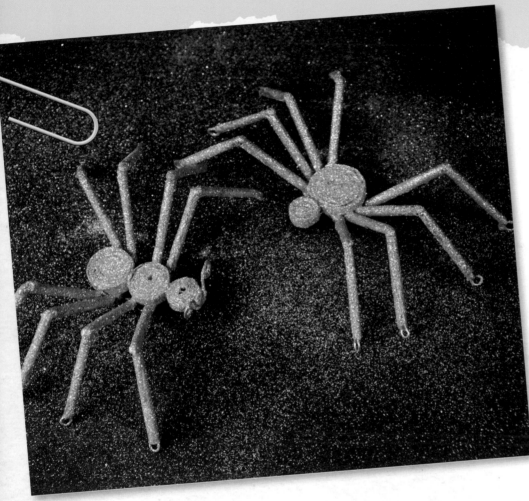

YOU'LL NEED:

+ Magazine pages
+ Magnets
+ Small gauge wire
+ Sulyn Silver glitter
+ Krylon Metallic Silver spray paints
+ Needle-nose pliers with wire cutter
+ Scissors
+ Elmer's Glue
+ E-6000 craft adhesive
+ Hot glue gun and glue sticks

SIZE: 4" x 6½" (100mm x 165mm)

HERE'S HOW:

1. Cut magazine pages into 1½" x 11" (40mm x 280mm) strips.

2. Roll them into tubes and glue the ends so they stay in place with a tiny dot of Elmer's. These will be for the body.

3. Grab the end of the tube with the tip of the pliers and twist the tube around it to create your disk.

4. Daub a dot of Elmer's on the end to keep it in place.

5. Make one large disk with 3 tubes and 1 small with one tube.

6. Glue a small disk to the large disk to create the body of the spider. Let dry.

7. Cut more magazine pages in 4" x 6" (100mm x 150mm) rectangles.

2

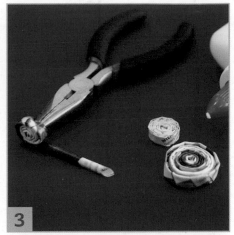

3

8. Roll them into tubes and glue the ends so they stay in place with a tiny dot of Elmer's. These are for the legs.

9. Make 16 of these tubes and cut them 1½" (40mm) long.

10. With the excess, you will cut 4 small 1" long tubes.

11. Cut 4 pieces of wire 7½" (190mm) long.

12. Bend one end of the wire into a loop and then string 2 leg pieces, one 1" (25mm) piece and then 2 more leg pieces on the wire and loop the wire again. Make 4.

13. Hot glue the 1" (25mm) pieces in the middle of your wired legs to one side of the body of the spider. This will be the underside.

5

6

14. Bend the legs in the shape you want and daub Elmer's Glue on the legs where the bends are to keep them in place. Let dry.

15. Spray paint with the Metallic Silver. Let dry.

16. Coat in more Elmer's Glue and cover in glitter. Let dry.

17. Adhere a magnet to the underside with E-6000 and let dry.

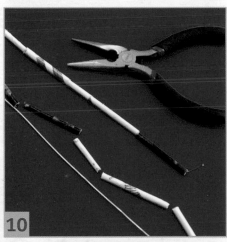

10

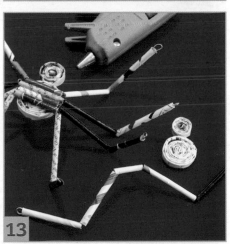

13

15

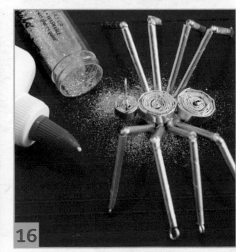

16

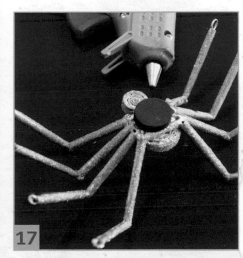

17

Black Diamonds

I've been wanting to use Extreme Glitter for a while, but just couldn't figure out exactly what to do with it and how to make it work for my particular take on crafting. These could be holiday ornaments if you wanted to change the color (just add a wash of color over the newspaper lining), but I quite like them just hanging around catching the light.

YOU'LL NEED:

- ✦ Cardboard
- ✦ Newspaper
- ✦ Sulyn Black glitter
- ✦ Plaid Black Extreme Glitter (2781)
- ✦ Krylon Black flat spray paint
- ✦ Clear filament (fishing line)
- ✦ Craft knife
- ✦ Cutting Mat
- ✦ Elmer's Glue
- ✦ Glue stick
- ✦ Hot glue gun and glue sticks

SIZE: 4½" x 6" (115mm x 150mm)

Combine Newspaper or Magazine Pages and Extreme Glitter on Ornaments!

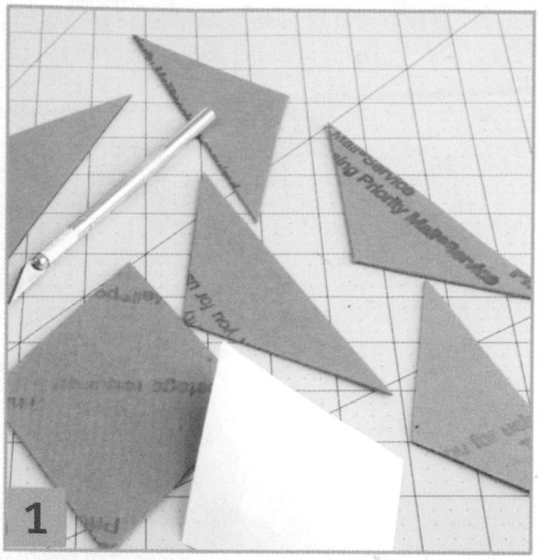

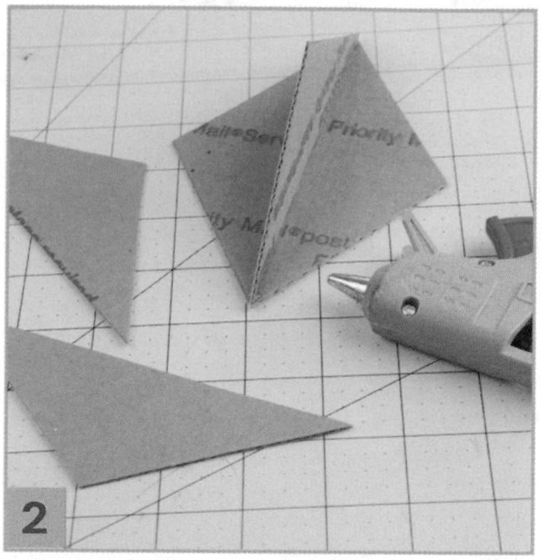

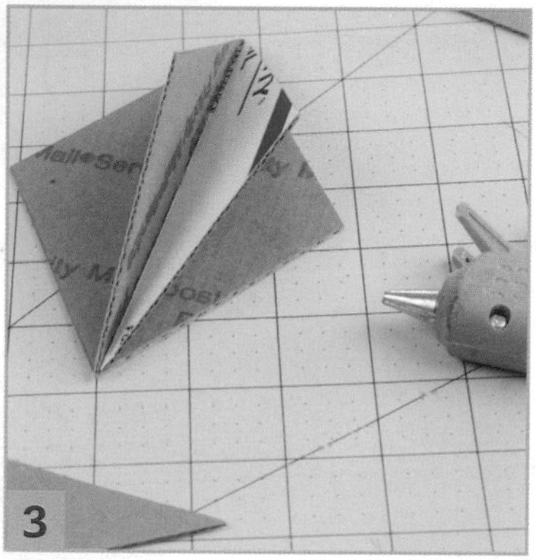

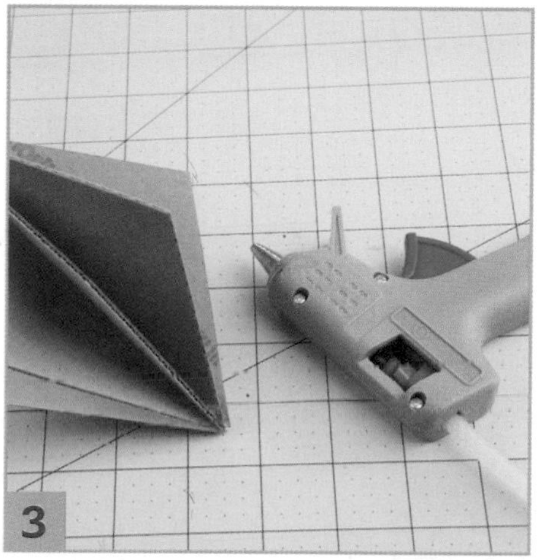

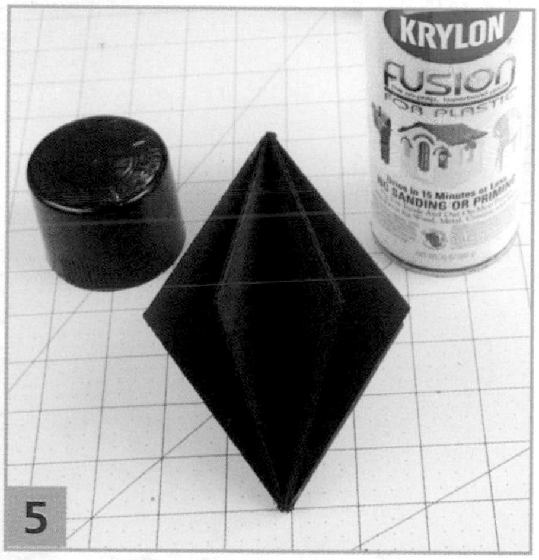

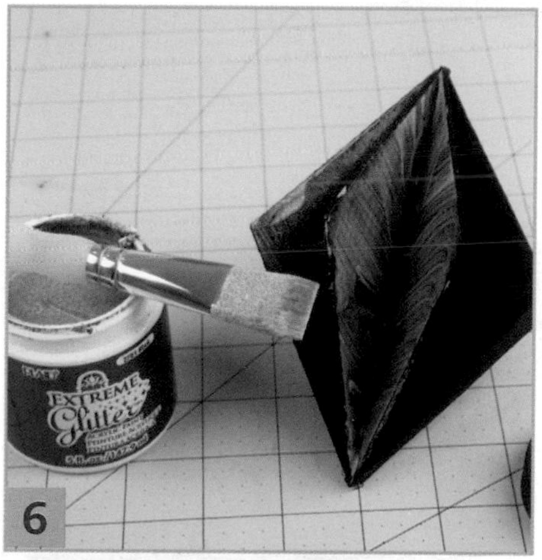

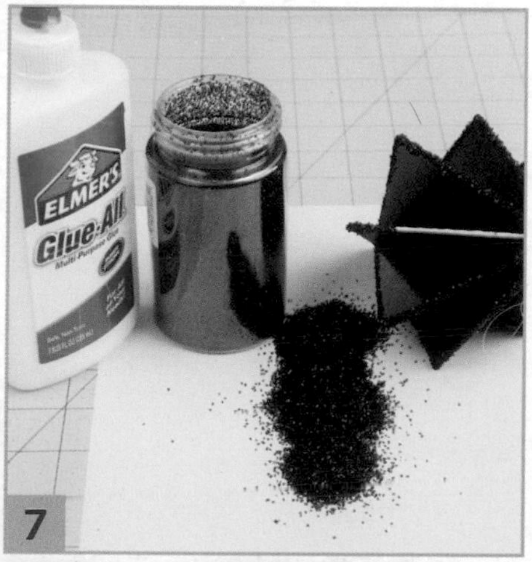

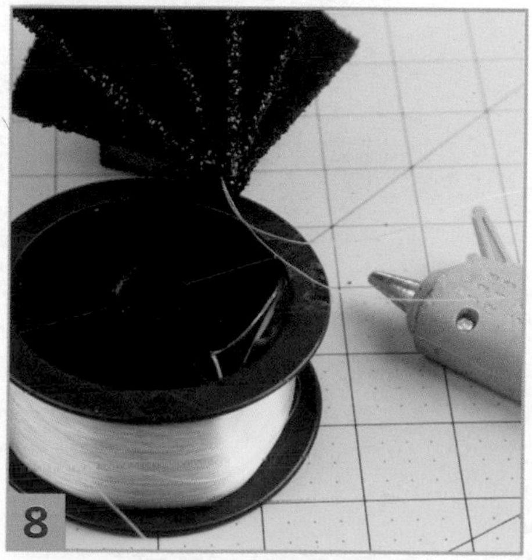

HERE'S HOW:

1. From cardboard, cut 1 diamond and 6 diamond halves.
2. Hot glue two halves crosswise on the whole diamond.
3. Glue a half in between each section.
4. Paint Elmer's Glue in each crevice for more support.
   Let dry.
5. Spray with the Black paint.
6. Coat with 2 layers of Extreme Glitter. Let dry.
7. Put a thin line of Elmer's Glue on each edge of the ornament and dip in loose black glitter.
8. Hot glue a loop of filament to the ornament for hanging.
9. Cover the hot glue in more glitter to disguise it.
10. Cut triangles from book pages, magazines or wrapping paper. Fold each in half. Use a glue stick to attach these shapes inside of each section.

❊ See project patterns on page 75

Decorative Lace Vase

Once I started playing with cardboard for this book I couldn't stop.

Gluing geometric shapes together to create things like vases and bowls was just too much fun. What an adrenaline rush the person who invented the first cardboard box must have felt! I always feel the same after a project like this. Tweak the pattern just a little and your shape changes. It's a blast!

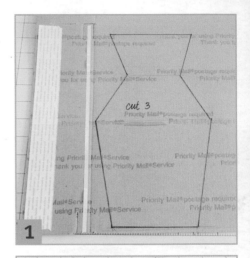

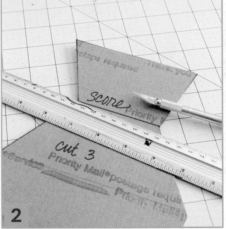

YOU'LL NEED:

- ✦ Cardboard
- ✦ Phone book pages, book pages or newspaper
- ✦ ¼ yard of lace (or a lace placemat)
- ✦ Plaid Mod Podge
- ✦ Krylon Fusion Black spray paint
- ✦ 1" (25mm)-wide paintbrush

- ✦ Craft knife
- ✦ Elmer's Glue
- ✦ Elmer's Spray Adhesive
- ✦ Blue painter's masking tape

SIZE: 4" x 4" x 4" (100mm x 100mm x 100mm) triangular base, 11" (280mm) tall

HERE'S HOW:

1. Cut out 3 cardboard vases and 1 base using the patterns.

2. Score the top part of your cardboard pieces on one side of each of the pieces. The lower score should be done on the opposite side of each cardboard piece. This is so they bend in different directions easily.

3. Tape the pieces together so they create the shape of the vase.

4. Squeeze glue where the edges meet so that it's sturdy.

5. Flip the vase over on its mouth and glue on the base. Let the entire structure dry.

6. Cut out strips of phone book pages, book pages or newspaper.

7. Using slightly watered down glue, start adhering strips of book pages to cover the entire vase and inside the mouth. Apply several layers of book pages so it's hefty. Let dry.

8. Using spray adhesive, lightly coat one side of the lace and gently press to your vase.

9. Spray the lace with the Black spray paint and remove the lace. The lace is your stencil and the spray adhesive keeps it in place. Do this on each side of the vase. Let dry.

10. Coat the entire vase with Mod Podge to make it even more sturdy.

If you're feeling super crafty, try the lace cuff technique on page 34 using 2 different colors of spray paint. It gives a terrific effect.

✳ See project patterns on page 76

Lace on a Vase, Oh My!

Paper Flower Keyholder

If you need a quick "just because" gift for someone, this is it! It's simple to make, couldn't be less expensive, and we can all use one. I, for one, am always losing my keys and this is the easiest way for me to keep track of them. I just plop them on the hook the minute I get inside the front door. Oh, and it's pretty.

YOU'LL NEED:

- ✦ Wire hanger
- ✦ Book pages
- ✦ Small piece of cardboard
- ✦ Krylon Clear Coat
- ✦ Scissors
- ✦ Stapler
- ✦ Needle-nose pliers with a built in wire cutter
- ✦ Hot glue gun
- ✦ glue sticks

SIZE: 5" (125mm) diameter

'Just Because' Gift

Here's how:

1. Cut out a cardboard circle that is a bit larger than a quarter.

2. Cut your wire hanger 10" (25cm) long and bend it as shown in the photo. It should have a hook and an area where you can glue it down to your flat circle of cardboard.

3. Use pliers to form a tiny loop at each end of your wire to give it a finished look.

4. Hot glue the wire on top of the circle of cardboard. Be generous with the glue because it will be covered by the flower.

5. Cut out 6 layers of book pages using the flower pattern provided (or make up your own).

6. Staple the layers together in the middle in an X. (This is my big flower making secret.)

7. Optional: For the inside of the flower, cut a 1" x 5" (25mm x 125mm) strip of book page like fringe. Roll it up and glue it in the center.

8. Fold up the top layer to cover the staples and continue folding up the layers to make your flower come to life.

9. Lightly spray with Clear Coat and let dry.

10. Give it several more coats of Clear Coat, but only a little at a time. Do this until the flower is sturdy.

11. Hot glue the flower on top of the wire and disk and hang with a nail.

✳ See project pattern on page 76.

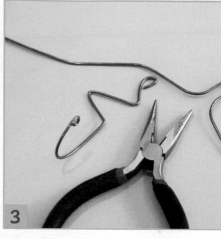

Mona Lisa Briefcase

I kept seeing these hard briefcases from the 1980s all over town for no more than a couple of dollars and I decided it was time to grab one and see what I could do with it. Well, it sat around for a year before I started covering it in book pages. It sat around for almost another year before I was struck by some terrific stencil art on a street post. It's amazing how you can be crossing the street and get inspiration from something out of left field. I hunted for images on the internet, printed them on book pages and glued them right down. Now I have the smirkiest briefcase in town. Is smirkiest a word? Well, it is now.

YOU'LL NEED:

- Hard briefcase or small piece of hard luggage
- Book pages
- Cool graphic image (I've included the Mona Lisa for you, just enlarge her as desired)
- Plaid Mod Podge Gloss
- Xerox printer at the copy shop (Don't use your home printer - the ink will run.)
- Scissors, Sandpaper
- Elmer's Glue, glue stick

Size: 13" x 18" (330mm x 460mm)

HERE'S HOW:

1. Clean all dirt from your briefcase and rough up the surface with sandpaper so that the book pages will stick.

2. Cut up some book pages and adhere them with Elmer's Glue.

3. Mona Lisa Image: Glue book pages together to create an 8½" x 11" (215mm x 280mm) sheet of paper. Enlarge the Mona Lisa (or your graphic image) so that 3 of them fit on your case. Place the image on the copy machine and run your book page paper through the printer. You now have a Mona Lisa printed on your book pages.

4. Cut out the image and make 3 copies at the copy shop. It will be easier to adhere to your briefcase if it's a Xerox copy.

5. Cut out the images and glue them on to the briefcase. Let dry.

6. Cover the whole case in several coats of Mod Podge.

✳ See project artwork on page 74 or create your own!

Smirkiest Briefcase in Town

Office Folder Book Page Coasters

I was that guy who got fired from every office job because I was in the back playing with the copy machine instead of doing my work. Ok, it worked out for me because now all I do every day is play with copy machines and make stuff. The scary thought is that it would have been tragic if all of that experimenting had gone to waste. Now I get to share my office experimenting with all of you. I even let my assistants play on the copy machine when they are feeling the urge. It's the least I can do, don't you think?

YOU'LL NEED:

- ✦ Images you want to use
- ✦ Transparent plastic office folders in different colors (Note: page protectors are too flimsy for this project)
- ✦ Book pages
- ✦ Copy machine (I used my home machine for these)

- ✦ Drinking glass
- ✦ Sewing machine with a heavy duty denim or leather needle (you are sewing through plastic)
- ✦ Pinking shears

- ✦ Glue stick (If your copy machine only accepts 8½" x 11" (215mm x 280mm) pages, glue some book pages together.)

SIZE: 4" (100mm) diameter

HERE'S HOW:

1. Cut out some book pages that are about 5" x 7"(125mm x 175mm). [If your copy machine only accepts 8½" x 11" (215mm x 280mm) paper, glue some pages together to bring the page up to size.]

2. Place your images on a copy machine making sure they are far enough apart so that you can cut a circle around them.

3. Place the book pages in the copy machine so that you print the images on each page over the text. (This is my secret double print technique.)

4. Cut a circle around the image. The top rim of a drinking glass works well as a pattern for this.

5. Cut out 2 circles from the plastic folder that are larger than your book page circle.

6. Insert your printed image and sew around it with the sewing machine.

7. Trim the edges with pinking sheers.

8. Repeat until you have an entire set.

✱ Use artwork on page 70 & 71 or create your own!

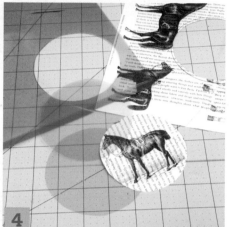

detail

Accordion Card

I'm always on the hunt for accordion post cards when I travel to new places. There's something about a long string of images that gets me very excited. More than that, I think they look super fun pinned to a wall—much better than just one little post card, don't you think?I know you can come up with different images to make this project your own. I bet if you dig through your images you'll find some favorites to put on your home copy machine for this project.Oh, one more thing, I'm sure you noticed that I like to recycle my cereal boxes for the cards. They're the perfect weight for this project. My guess is you've already figured that one out yourself—being the creative person you are!

YOU'LL NEED:

- ✦ Cereal box to cut up for your cards
- ✦ Book pages
- ✦ Images to copy on your home copy machine
- ✦ Several sheets of plain copy paper

- ✦ Ribbon
- ✦ Scissors
- ✦ 1" (25mm) wide paintbrush
- ✦ Elmer's Glue

SIZE: 5" x 6" (125mm x 150mm)

Tie this up with some ribbon and send it to your favorite person in a handmade stitched book page envelope. Learn how on page 57.

HERE'S HOW:

1. Cut 4 equal sized cards from your cereal box. Make sure the cards are 1" (25mm) smaller than the book pages you're gluing on top of them or you'll have to use more than one book page per card—which is fine, but more work.

2. Using slightly watered down glue, adhere your book pages to the printed side of the cereal card leaving ½" (15mm) of the book page exposed all the way around.

3. Cut the book page at an angle on each corner as shown. Cover with some glue and fold over to the back. This will give your card a wonderful clean finish.

4. Cut the plain pages just a bit smaller than the cereal card and glue to the back of the card. (This is where you'll be writing.)

5. Copy images, cut them out and glue them over your book pages. I dry my cards between some heavy books to keep them flat.

6. Cut a 1" (25mm) wide strip of plain paper the width of your cards. Glue just a little less than ½" (15mm) on each card so they are connected. Do this to connect all 4 cards.

7. Fold up, wrap with a ribbon and send it off into the world.

Stitched Envelopes

One of my favorite things to do is sew paper. My second favorite thing to do is to pick up damaged books on the street and give them another life. Pair those together and you get these lovely envelopes (which, by the way, also make a terrific gift in sets of 10). People will appreciate that you took the time to make them something special that they can actually use. The bonus is you'll definitely get one back in the mail when they send you a thank you card. Is that so wrong?

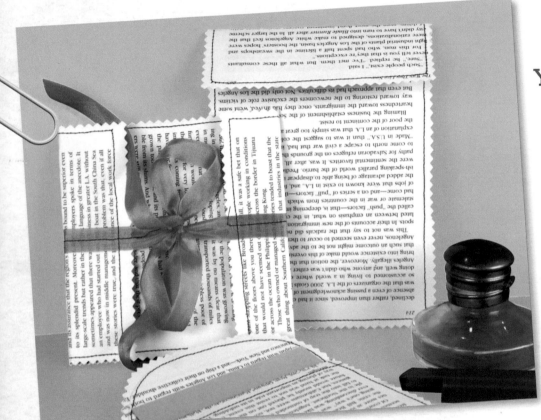

YOU'LL NEED:

✦ 4 book pages per envelope

✦ Seam tape in a color you like

✦ Sewing machine with Black or Red thread

✦ Pinking shears

✦ Glue sticks

SIZE: 5" x 7" (125mm x 175mm)

One of My Favorite Things

HERE'S HOW:

PLAIN ENVELOPE

1. Cut out 4 book pages and trim them all the same size. Each side of your envelope will be 2 pages thick so it's stong.

2. Cut 2 of the 4 pages about 1½" (15mm) shorter than the other two.

3. Stitch across the top of each shorter page with your sewing machine.

4. Cut above that stitch with your pinking shears.

5. Place that stitched page on the larger pages and stitch around the entire envelope.

6. Pink around all the edges.

7. Fold the flap over and seal with a glue stick once you're ready to send it off.

detail

Plain Envelope

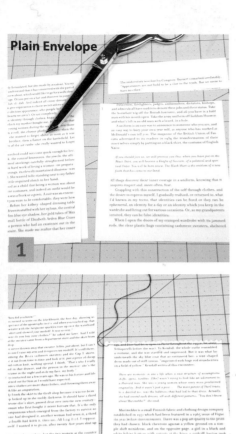

1

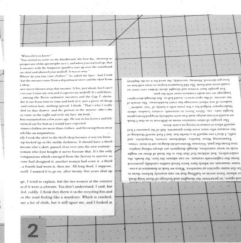

2

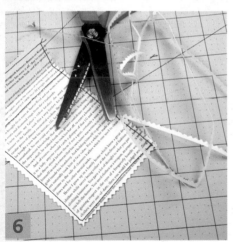

3 & 4

5

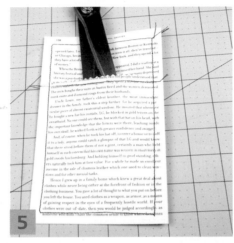

6

Ribbon Envelope

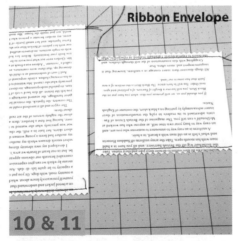

10 & 11

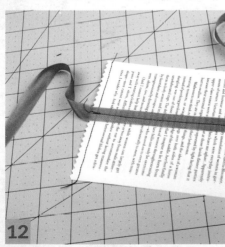

12

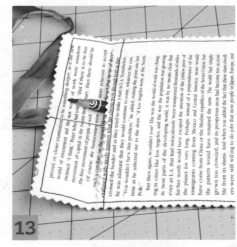

13

RIBBON ENVELOPE

8. Cut out 4 book pages and trim them all the same size

9. Cut 2 of the book pages about 3" (75mm) shorter than the other two.

10. Stitch on the top and bottom of the shorter pages and the top and bottom of the larger page.

11. Pink the edges just above where you stitched

12. Stitch the seam tape down the center of the larger piece.

13. Place the smaller piece in the middle of the larger piece with the seam tape on the outside and stitch down the sides.

14. Fold the flaps over and tie.

Printed Mini Journals

Not sure if you're like me, but I always have an idea that I want to jot down, so I enjoy having a cool little idea book hanging around. I started to make these with all of the copies I had left over from my projects because one side was always blank. Pretty soon my friends started asking for them so I got a little more creative. I find this version the easiest and most inspiring to make. They are a great guest gift at a dinner party, too. Just wrap it in some ribbon and put one on each person's plate. They will love it, I promise.

YOU'LL NEED:

- ✦ Book pages
- ✦ Cardstock in 1 or 2 colors
- ✦ Random images you like
- ✦ Blank paper from your printer or a notebook
- ✦ Home printer
- ✦ Large office stapler

SIZE: 4¼" x 5" (110mm x 125mm)

I Love
Mini Journals

HERE'S HOW:

1. Cut out some book pages that are at least 5" x 8" (125mm x 200mm) in size.

2. Toss some random images on your copy machine.

3. Feed the book pages through the machine to create some inspirational image pages to place throughout your book. Make about 5 different image pages.

4. Journal cover: Pick your favorite image page and put that on the copy machine and feed your cardstock through the printer. Fold the cover in half and then unfold. The fold line will be your guide for the binding staples.

5. Cut all of your images and extra paper 5" x 7¾" (125mm x 195mm) in size.

6. Stack all of the pages together with the cardstock cover as the top layer.

7. Staple twice in the fold to bind your mini journal.

8. Fold your book in half and you're done.

✳ Use artwork on pages 67 & 69 or create your own!

Butterfly Obelisk

When I first started making this project I wanted to cover it in something really interesting but couldn't think of anything that would work better than phone book pages and butterflies. I have so many phone books hanging around it was time to do something with them other than prop myself up at the dinner table.

I'd much rather look for a number on this obelisk than in a floppy 45-pound phone book.

YOU'LL NEED:

- ✦ Cardboard
- ✦ Phone book or old book pages
- ✦ Black and White copies of butterflies
- ✦ Plaid Mod Podge Gloss
- ✦ 1" (25mm) wide paintbrush
- ✦ Craft knife
- ✦ Ruler
- ✦ Pencil
- ✦ Elmer's Glue
- ✦ Blue painter's masking tape

SIZE: 4" x 4" (100mm x 100mm) base, 13" (330mm) tall

✱ See project patterns on page 78

HERE'S HOW:

1. Enlarge the patterns provided as desired. As long as you enlarge at all the same percentage you'll be fine and all the pieces will fit together perfectly.

2. Cut out the shapes in cardboard.

3. Using a craft knife, lightly score along the dotted lines so that you can easily fold your pieces. Be careful not to cut all the way through the cardboard.

4. Tape the shapes together to form your obelisk.

5. Apply glue where the cardboard is touching to make your obelisk sturdy.

6. Cut strips of a phone book or book pages and apply with slightly watered down glue to the obelisk with the paintbrush. Let dry.

7. Laser copy the butterflies in this book at a copy shop. Don't use your home computer printer because the ink will run.

8. Cut out your black and white butterfly copies and glue them to the obelisk. Let dry.

9. Coat with Mod Podge for a beautiful finish.

✳ Use artwork on page 70 or create your own!

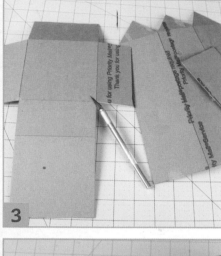

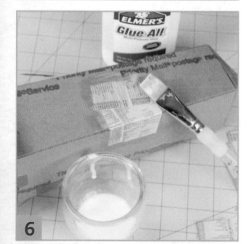

Butterflies Make Me Happy

Matting with Blown Ink

Why not spruce up a simple picture mat with some book pages. Hey, splatter some ink on it and you'll have a piece of art that will make people talk! This process makes a simple photograph or print more exciting and the entire piece becomes a work of art. It's a great way to contrast a modern technique with an antique look.

Try it with different colors of ink and see what happens.

Spruce Up a Picture

YOU'LL NEED:

- Book pages
- Newspaper
- Cardboard
- Black Calligraphy ink
- Craft knife
- Small paper cup
- 1 drinking straw
- 1" (25mm) wide paintbrush
- Transparent tape
- Elmer's Glue

SIZE: 9" x 12" (230mm x 305mm)

HERE'S HOW:

1. Decide how large you want your mat and window.

2. Cut the mat from cardboard.

3. Randomly cut your book pages. Depending on the size of the mat, you should be fine with about 5 pages.

4. Squirt some glue in a cup and water it down a tiny bit. This thins the glue so it's easy to spread.

5. Paint the glue on the cardboard and start adhering the book page pieces. Let dry.

6. Place the mat on large pieces of newspaper. Drip the ink in the corners and blow through the straw toward the center of the mat.

7. Cut out the center window of your mat to fit the image you're framing.

8. Center your image and tape it to the back of the mat, then complete your framing process.

✳ Use artwork on page 68 or create your own!

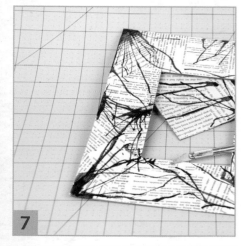

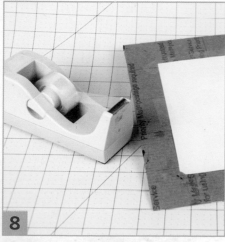

detail

Mini Silhouettes

Silhouettes have been around for centuries and I like to use them for everything from greeting cards to artwork.

This process is so easy and once you master it, you'll be making silhouettes out of everything you can toss on your copy machine! Let's just keep this process our little secret, okay?

YOU'LL NEED:

- ✦ Frame
- ✦ Images that you think would make a great silhouette
- ✦ Book pages
- ✦ Black paper for matting
- ✦ Copy machine
- ✦ Craft knife
- ✦ Glue stick

❋ SIZE: 1½" x 2½" (40mm x 65mm) for silhouette only

HERE'S HOW:

1. Select your images. I used a *Dover* Clip Art book of animals for my images.

2. Cut out some book pages. Cut the edges so they are perfectly straight.

3. Put your image on your copy machine and run the book page through it so your image is printed directly on the book page.

4. Carefully cut around your image and turn it over. Voila!

5. Mount with a tiny bit of glue stick onto Black paper and frame.

✳ Use artwork on pages 70, 72 & 73 or create your own!

- -

SUPPLIERS FEATURED IN THIS BOOK:

Most craft and variety stores carry an excellent assortment of supplies. If you need something special, ask your local store to contact the following companies

- ✦ Xerox Copy Machines, Laser Printer
  Staples Copy Center, www.staples.com
- ✦ Table
  Ikea, www.ikea.com
- ✦ Glitter
  Plaid, www.plaidonline.com
  Sulyn, www.sulyn.com
- ✦ Mod Podge, Acrylic Paint
  Plaid, www.plaidonline.com

- ✦ Spray Paint, Spray Adhesive
  Krylon, www.krylon.com
- ✦ Artist Paintbrushes
  Royal, www.royalpaintbrushes.com
- ✦ Glue
  Elmer's, www.elmers.com
- ✦ Pinking Shears
  Fiskars, www.fiskars.com
- ✦ Images, Clip Art Books
  Dover

Artwork & Patterns

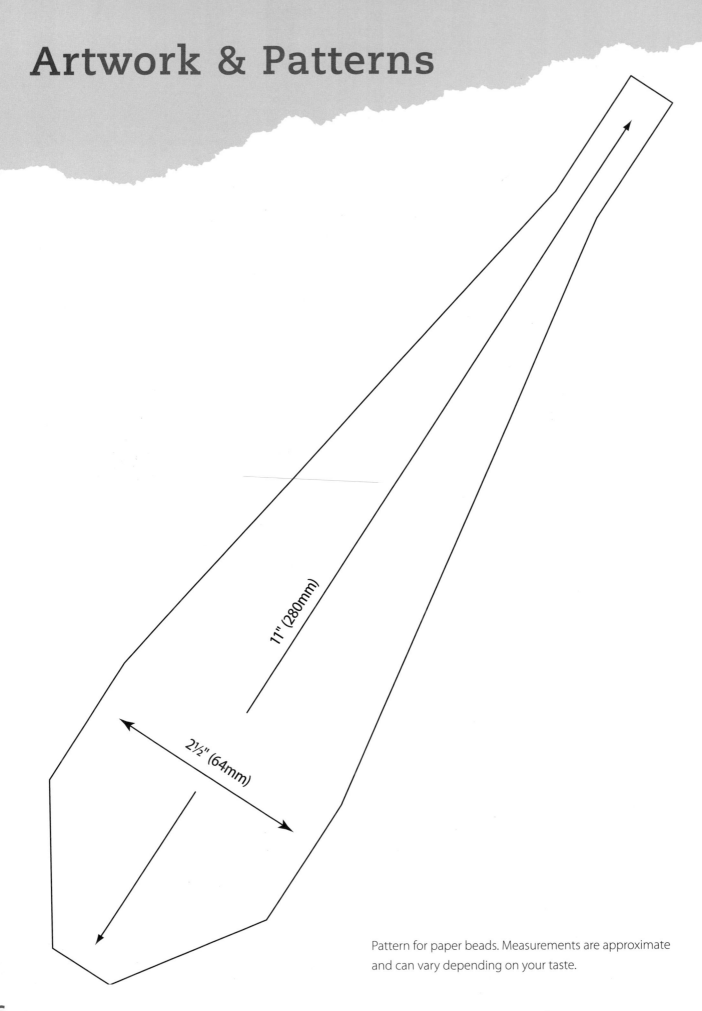

11" (280mm)

2½" (64mm)

Pattern for paper beads. Measurements are approximate and can vary depending on your taste.

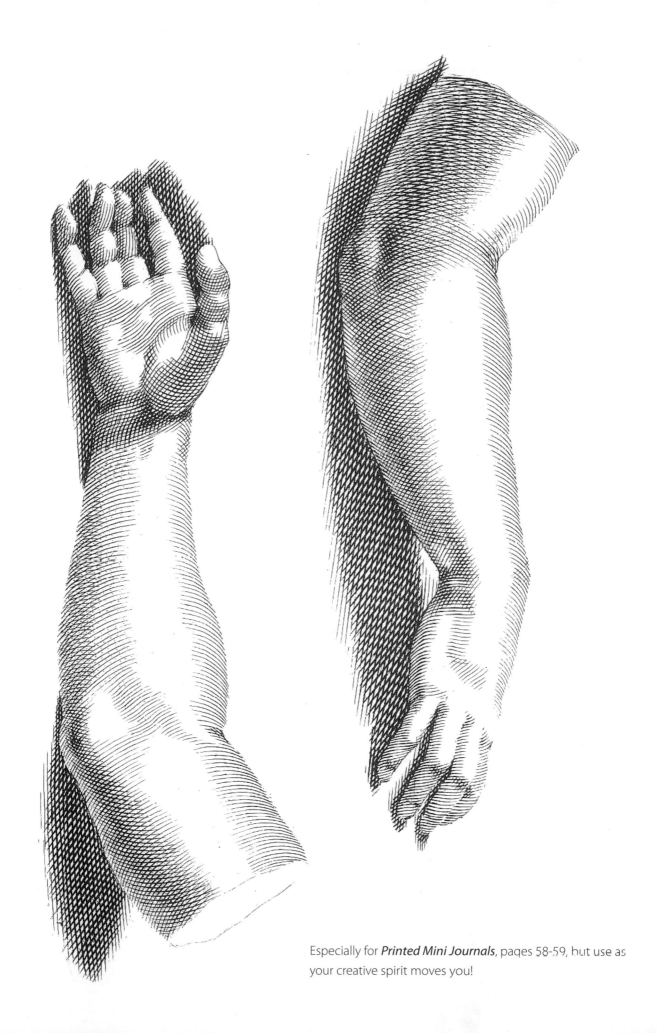

Especially for *Printed Mini Journals*, pages 58-59, but use as
your creative spirit moves you!

Especially for *Matting with Blown Ink*, pages 62-63, but use as your creative spirit moves you!

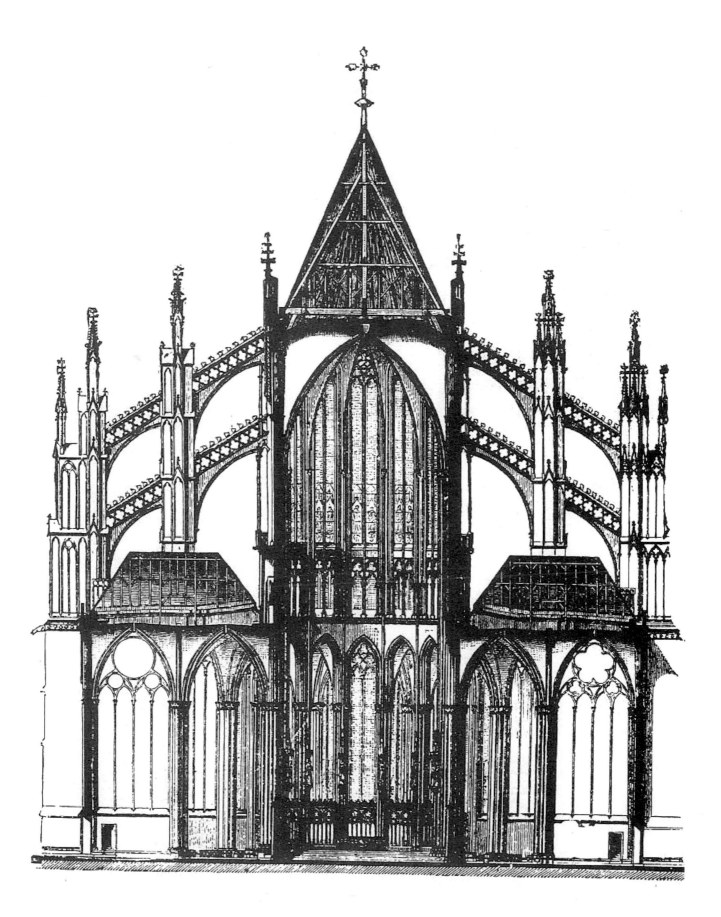

Especially for *Printed Mini Journals*, pages 58-59, but use as your creative spirit moves you!

Especially for *Mini Silhouettes*, pages 64-65, and *Butterfly Obelisk,* pages 60-61, *Office Folder Book Page Coasters*, pages 52-53, *3-D Greeting Card Box*, pages 24-25, *Book Page and Butterfly Table*, pages 22-23, but use as your creative spirit leads you!

Especially for *Office Folder Book Page Coasters*, pages 52-53, but use as your creative spirit moves you!

Especially for **Mini Silhouettes**, pages 64-65, but use as your creative spirit moves you!

Especially for *Mini Silhouettes*, pages 64-65, but use as your creative spirit moves you!

Especially for *Mona Lisa Briefcase*, pages 50-51, but use as your creative spirit moves you!

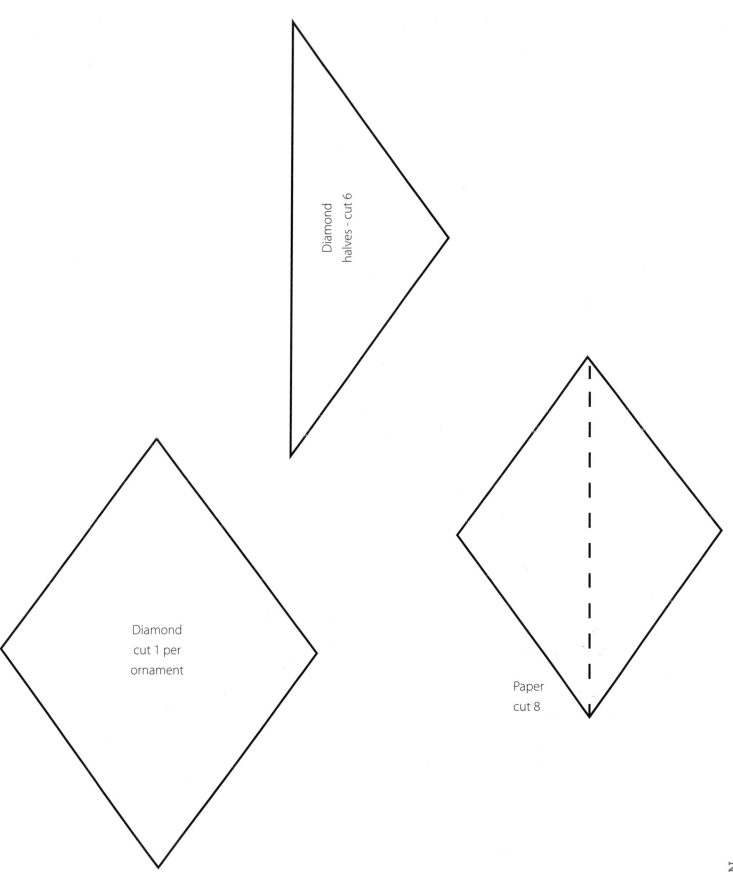

Diamond
halves - cut 6

Diamond
cut 1 per
ornament

Paper
cut 8

Pattern for **Black Diamonds**, page 44-45
Use at 100%

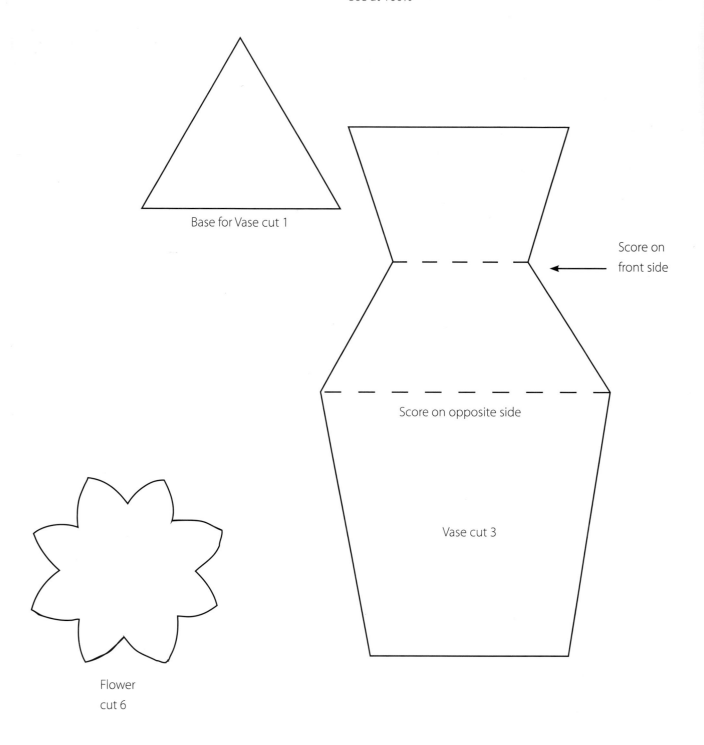

Patterns for *Decorative Lace Vase*, pages 46-47
Use at 100%

Base for Vase cut 1

Score on
front side

Score on opposite side

Vase cut 3

Flower
cut 6

Pattern for *Paper Flower Keyholder*, pages 48-49
Use at 150%

Patterns for *Masquerade Mask with Feathers*, pages 20-21
Use at 200%

Mask
cut 1

Patterns for *Sewn Flower Brooch and Cuff*, pages 32-33
Use at 100%

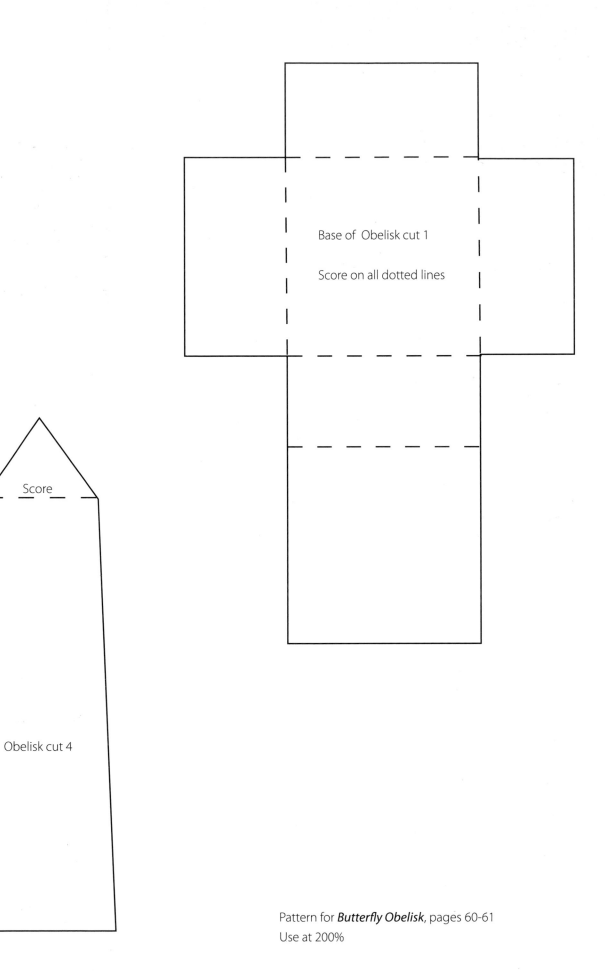

Base of Obelisk cut 1

Score on all dotted lines

Score

Obelisk cut 4

Pattern for *Butterfly Obelisk*, pages 60-61
Use at 200%

INDEX

ACQUISITION EDITOR: **Peg Couch**

COPY EDITOR: **Heather Stauffer**

COVER AND LAYOUT DESIGNER: **Ashley Millhouse**

DEVELOPMENTAL EDITOR: **Paul Hambke**

ASSISTANT EDITOR: **Katie Weeber**

PROOFREADER: **Lynda Jo Runkle**

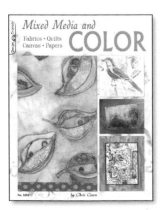